Rock Classics for Easy Guitar

CONTENTS

Page	Title	Artist
2	Are You Gonna Go My Way	*Lenny Kravitz*
5	Black Hole Sun	*Soundgarden*
9	Cat Scratch Fever	*Ted Nugent*
15	Crazy on You	*Heart*
22	Changes	*Jimi Hendrix*
24	Crazy Train	*Ozzy Osbourne*
28	Day Tripper	*The Beatles*
32	Eight Miles High	*The Byrds*
33	Flirtin' with Disaster	*Molly Hatchet*
38	Hot Blooded	*Foreigner*
42	I Don't Know	*Ozzy Osbourne*
46	Iron Man	*Black Sabbath*
49	Layla	*Derek and the Dominos*
53	Outshined	*Soundgarden*
58	Paradise City	*Guns N' Roses*
61	Rosanna	*Toto*
65	Runnin' with the Devil	*Van Halen*
68	S.A.T.O.	*Ozzy Osbourne*
71	Tightrope	*Stevie Ray Vaughan*
75	Welcome to the Jungle	*Guns N' Roses*
78	Walk This Way	*Aerosmith*
80	*Guitar Notation Legend*	

Cover photo by Lisa Sharken

ISBN 1-57560-656-9

Copyright © 2005 Cherry Lane Music Company
International Copyright Secured   All Rights Reserved

The music, text, design and graphics in this publication are protected by copyright law. Any duplication or transmission, by any means, electronic, mechanical, photocopying, recording or otherwise, is an infringement of copyright.

Visit our website at www.cherrylane.com

ARE YOU GONNA GO MY WAY

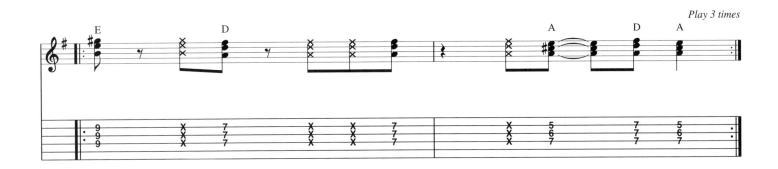
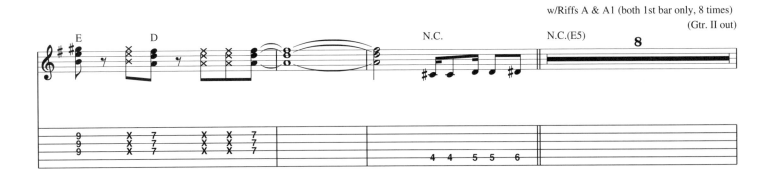
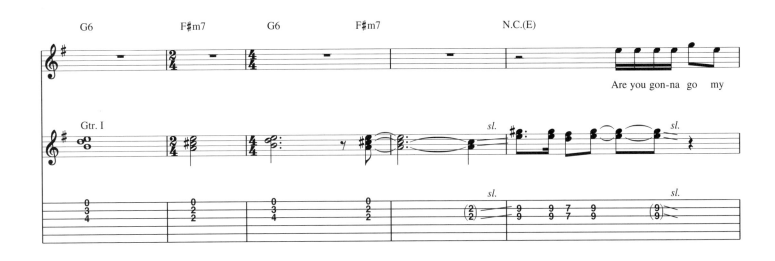
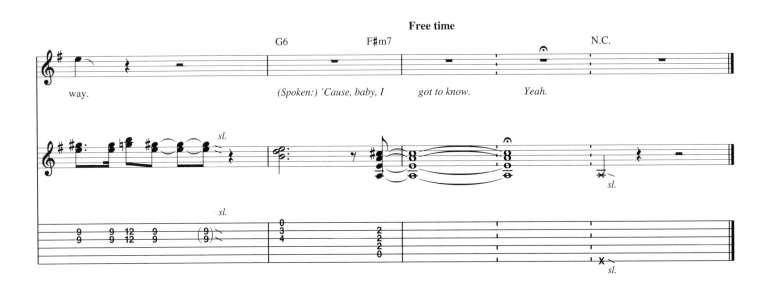

BLACK HOLE SUN

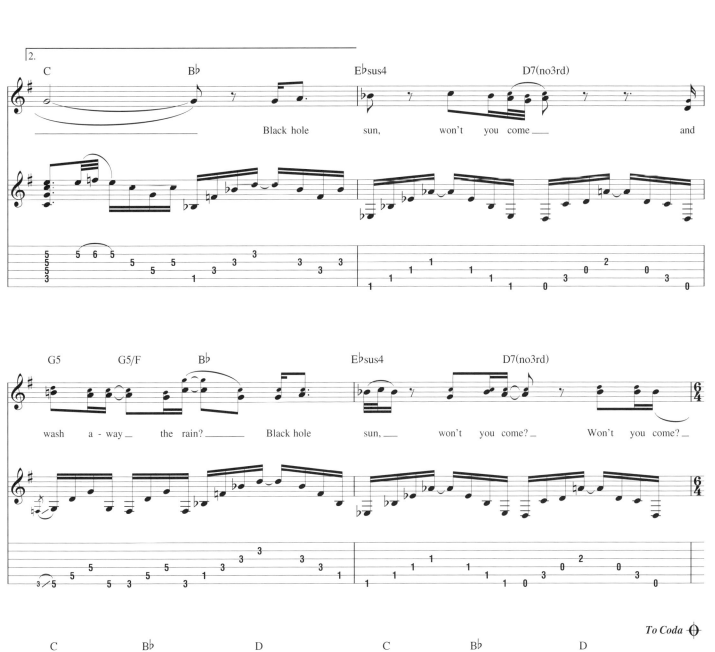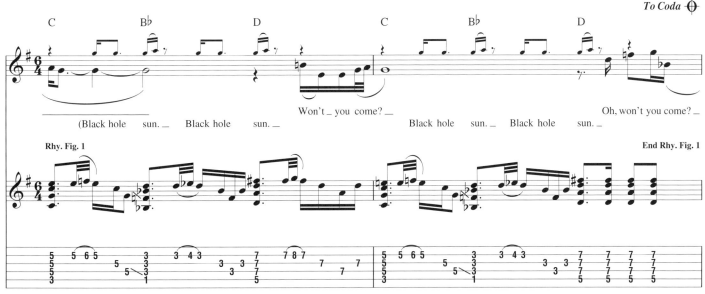

CAT SCRATCH FEVER

Words and Music by
Ted Nugent

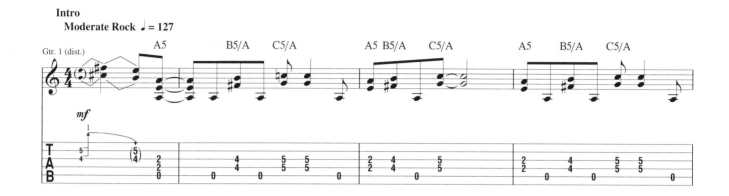

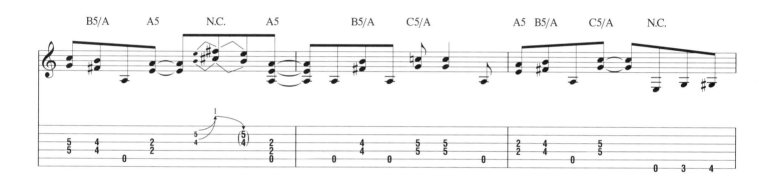

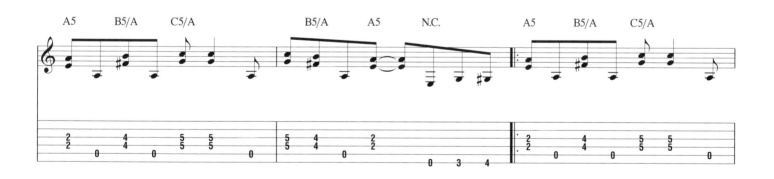

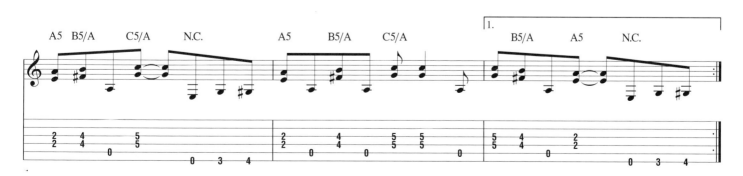

Copyright © 1977 by Magicland Music
All Rights Reserved   Used by Permission

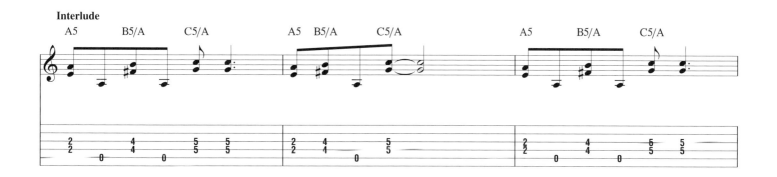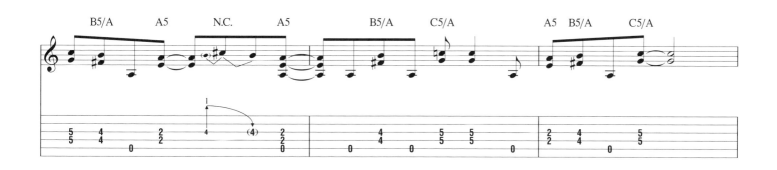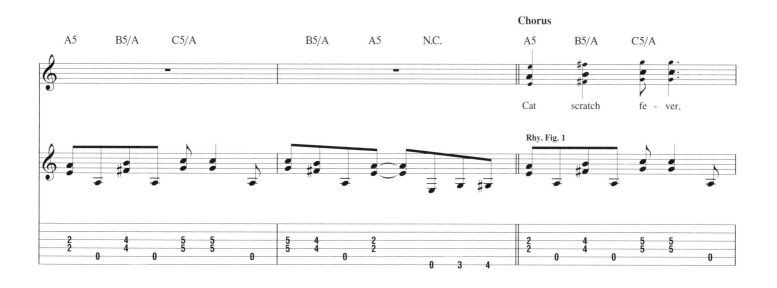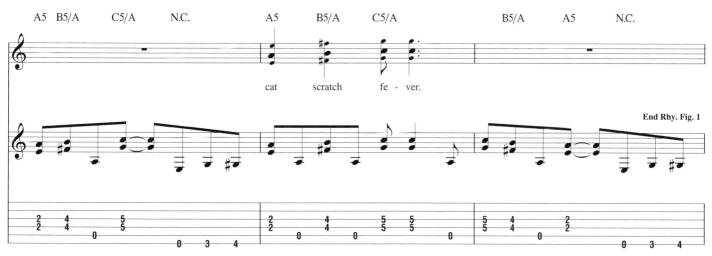

CRAZY ON YOU

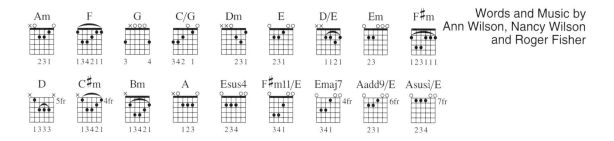

Words and Music by
Ann Wilson, Nancy Wilson
and Roger Fisher

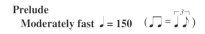

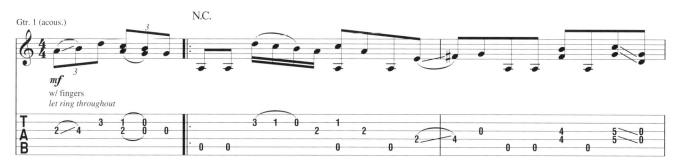

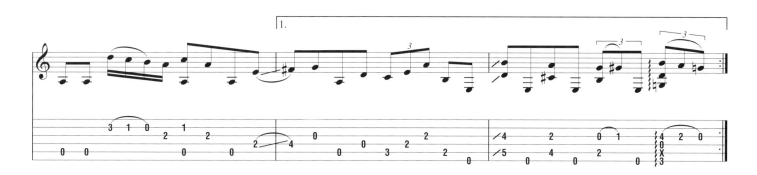

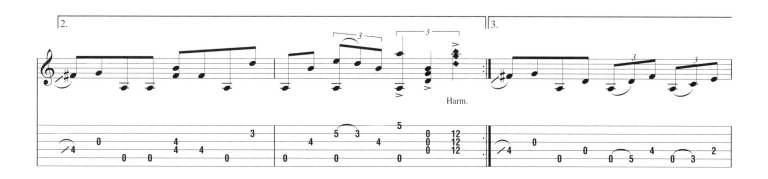

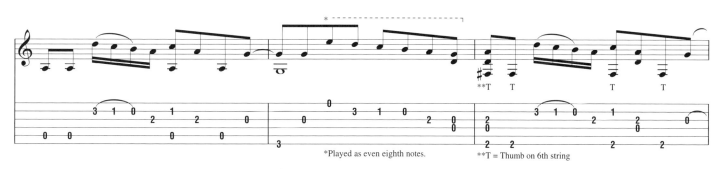

*Played as even eighth notes. **T = Thumb on 6th string

Copyright © 1976 Sony/ATV Tunes LLC
All Rights Administered by Sony/ATV Music Publishing, 8 Music Square West, Nashville, TN 37203
International Copyright Secured   All Rights Reserved

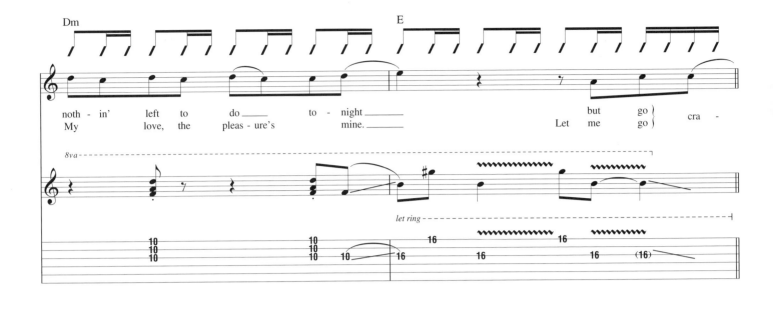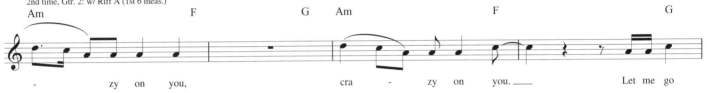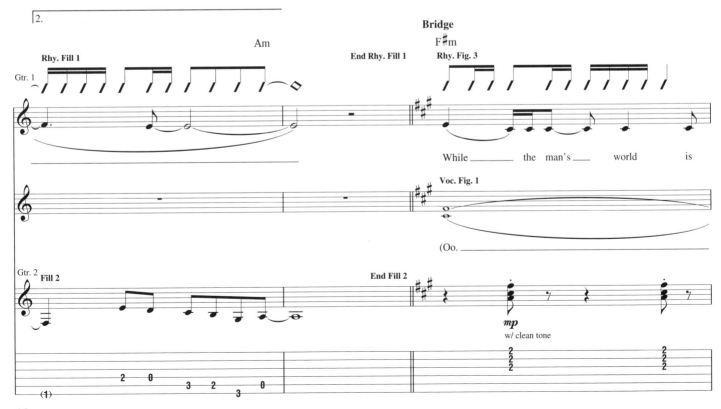

CHANGES

By Buddy Miles

Tune down 1/2 step:
(low to high) E♭-A♭-D♭-G♭-B♭-E♭

Intro
Moderate Rock ♩ = 116

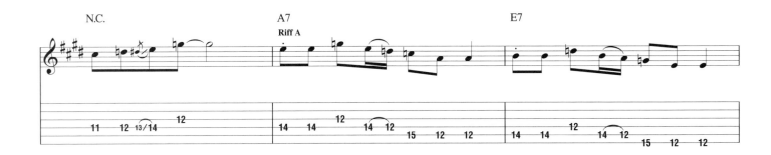
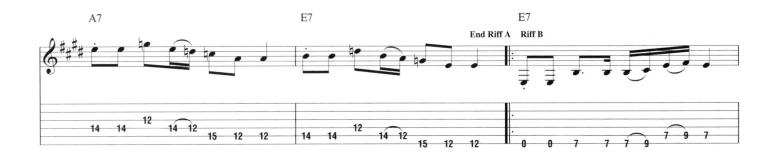
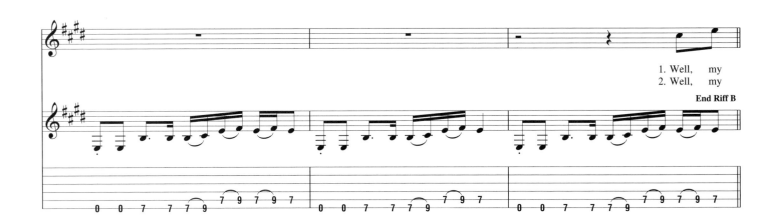

© 1967 (Renewed) Miles Ahead Music Publishing, Inc.
International Copyright Secured All Rights Reserved

CRAZY TRAIN

Words and Music by Ozzy Osbourne,
Randy Rhoads and Bob Daisley

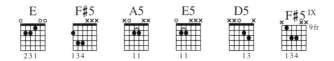

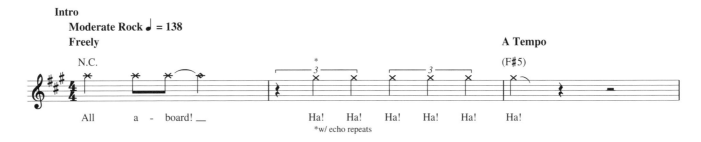

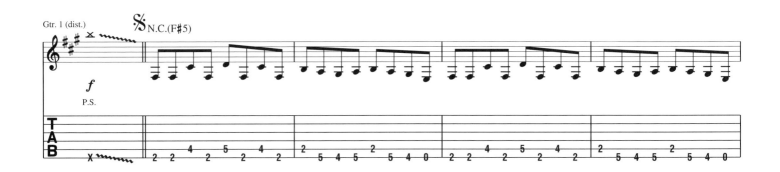

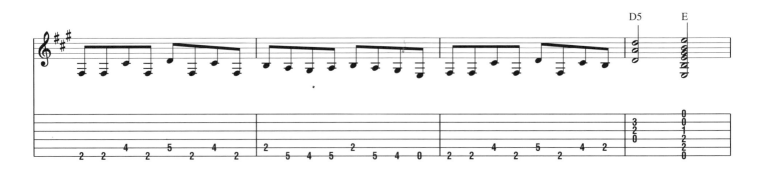

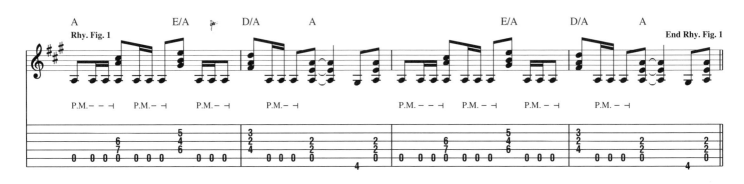

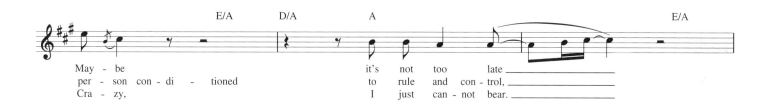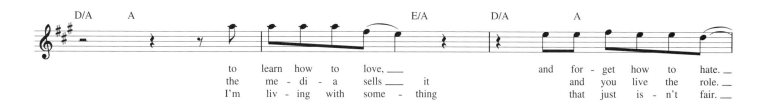

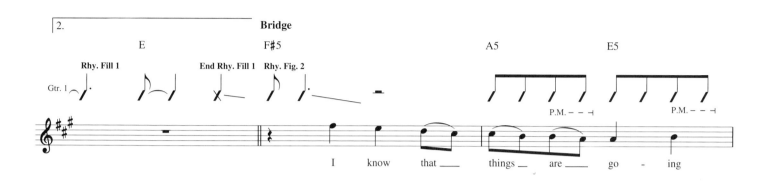
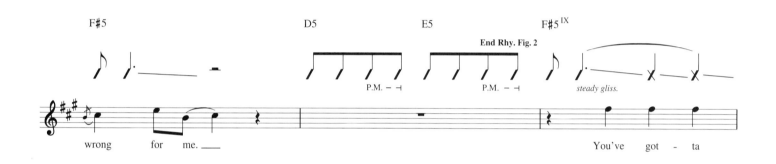
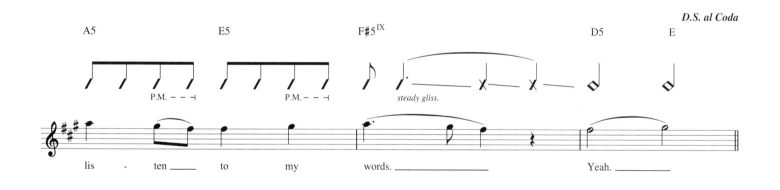
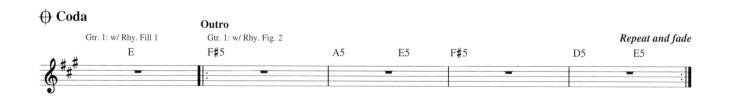

27

DAY TRIPPER

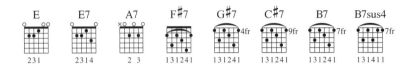

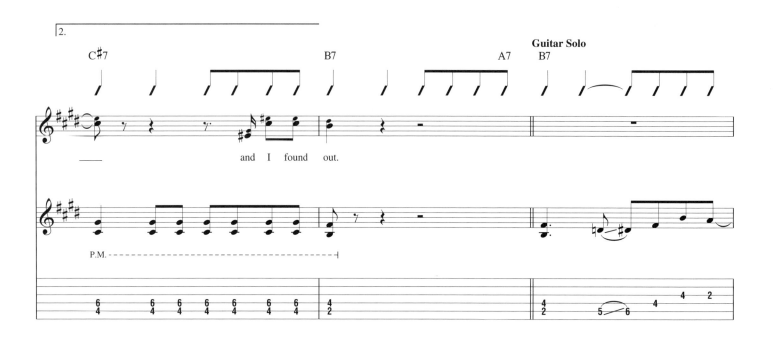
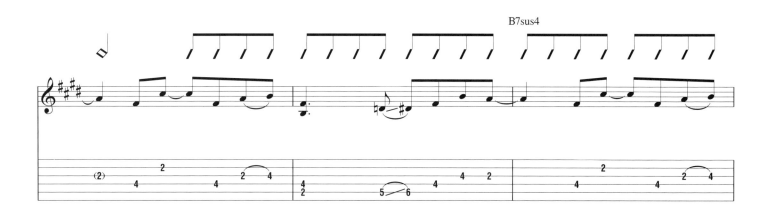
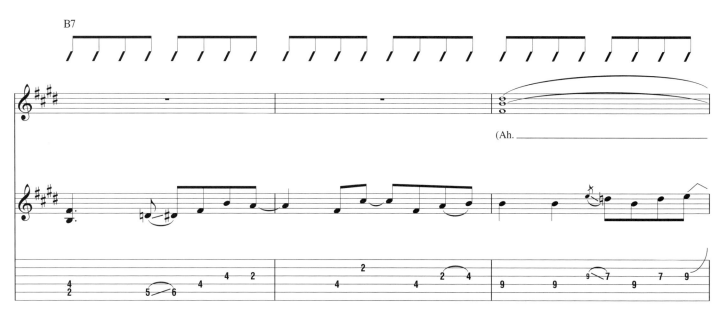

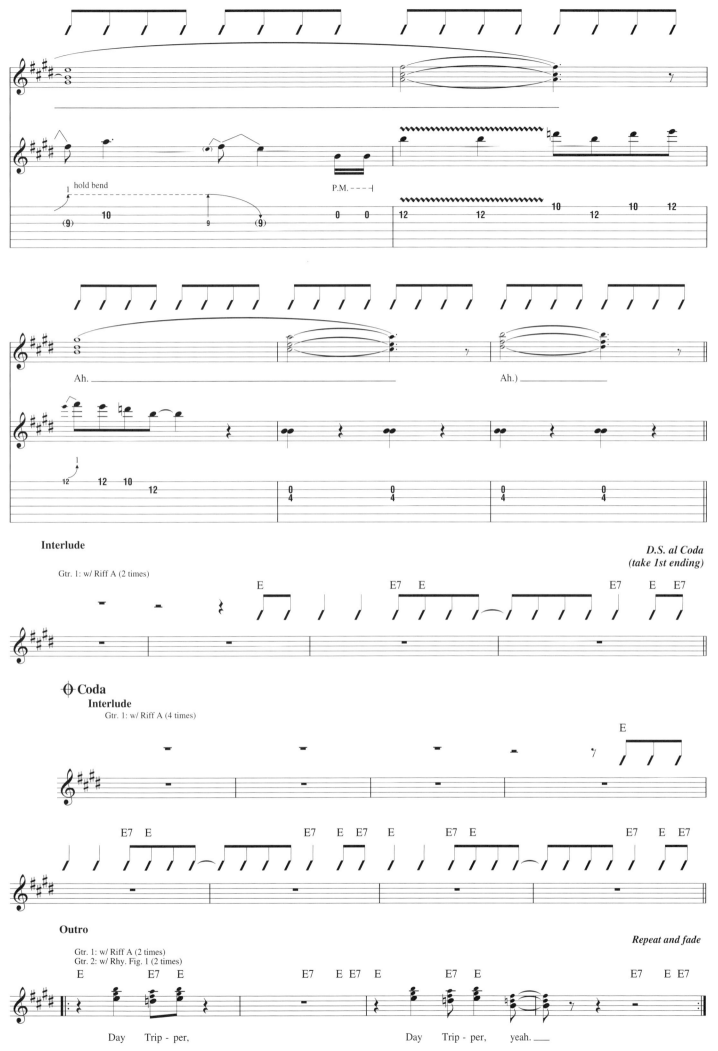

FLIRTIN' WITH DISASTER

**Words and Music by
David Lawrence Hlubek, Banner Harvey Thomas
and Danny Joe Brown**

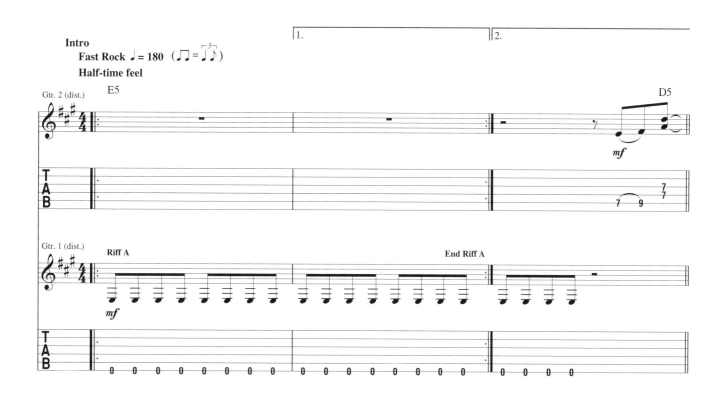

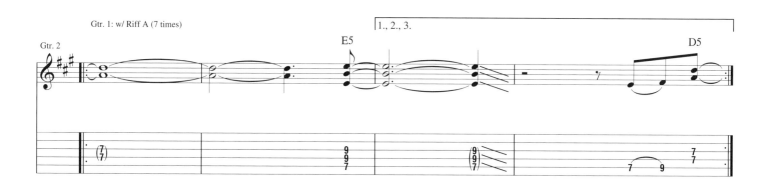

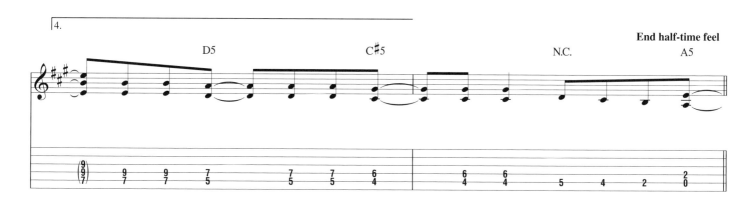

Copyright © 1979 MISTER SUNSHINE MUSIC, INC. (BMI)
International Copyright Secured   All Rights Reserved

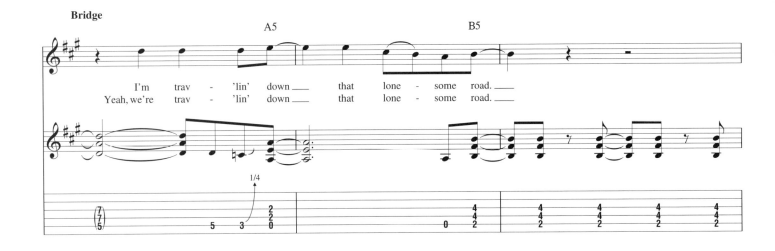
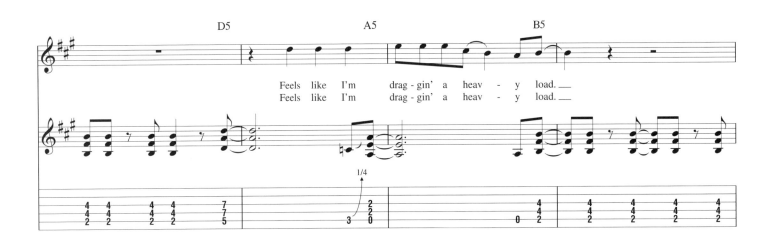

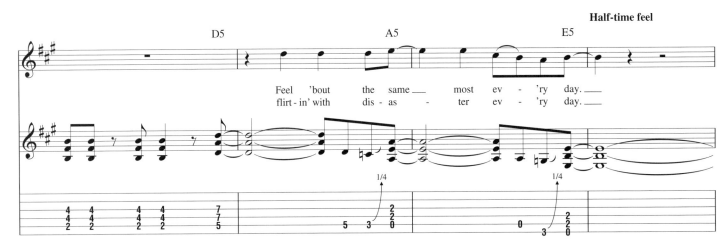

HOT BLOODED

Words and Music by
Mick Jones and Lou Gramm

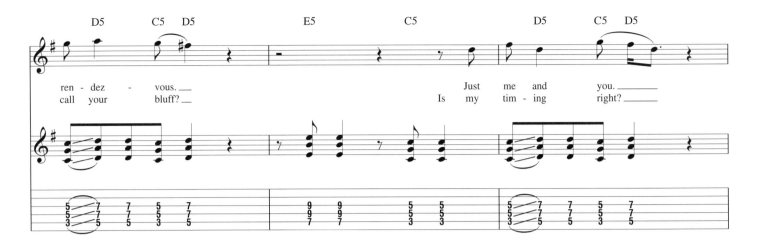
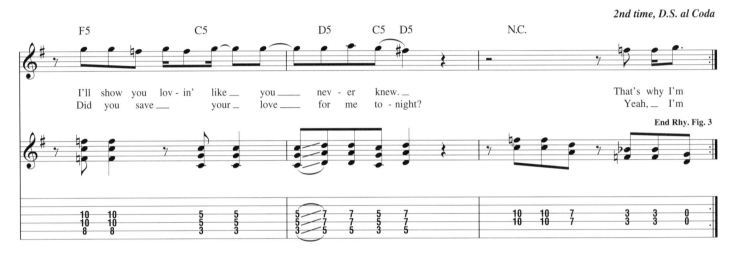

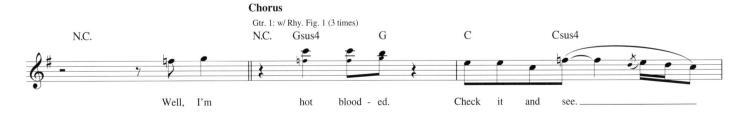

I DON'T KNOW

Words and Music by Ozzy Osbourne,
Randy Rhoads and Bob Daisley

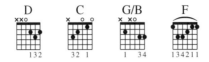

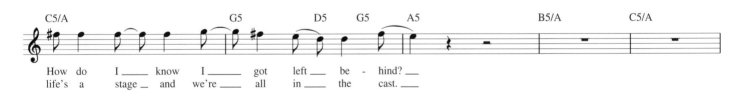

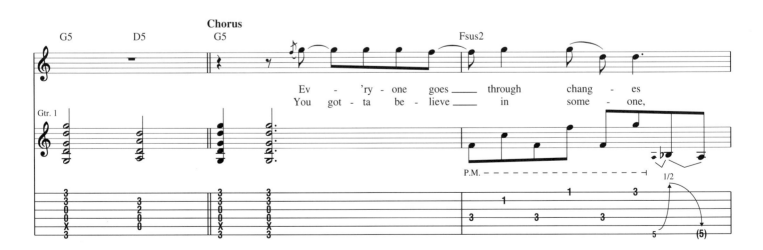

42

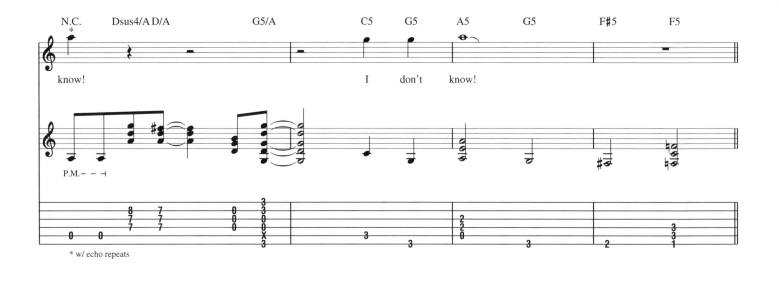
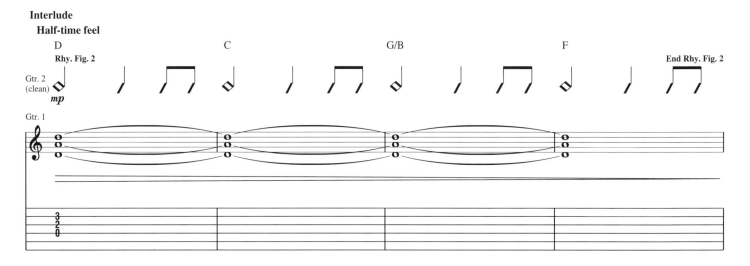

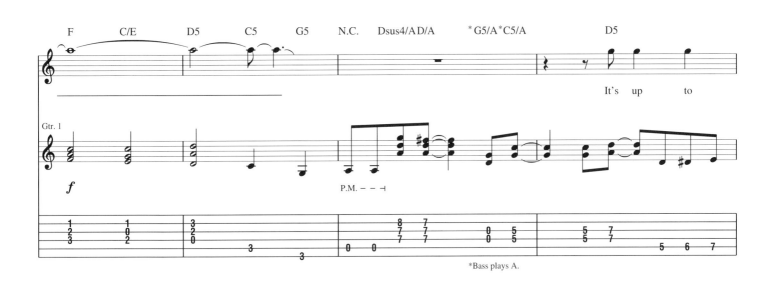
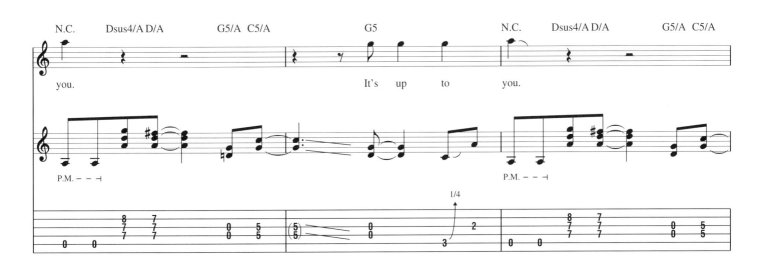
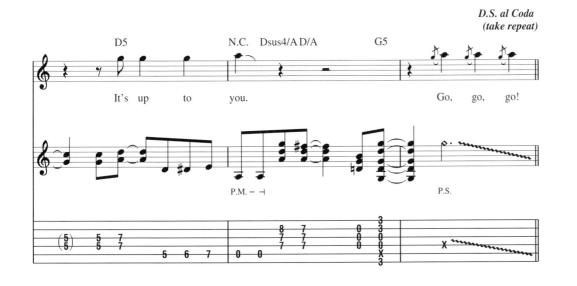

IRON MAN

Words and Music by
Frank Iommi, John Osbourne, William Ward
and Terence Butler

© Copyright 1970 (Renewed) and 1974 (Renewed) Westminster Music Ltd., London, England
TRO - Essex Music International, Inc., New York, controls all publication rights for the U.S.A. and Canada
International Copyright Secured
All Rights Reserved Including Public Performance For Profit
Used by Permission

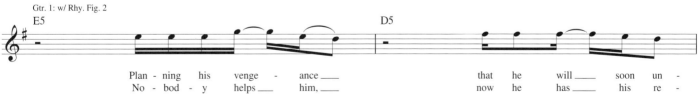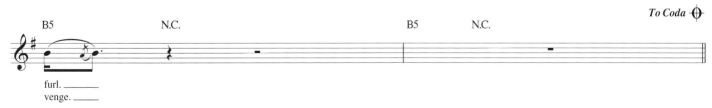

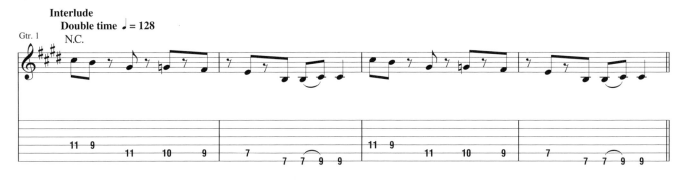

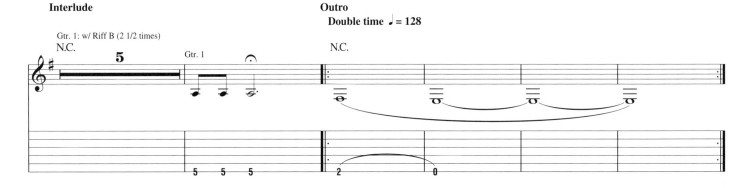

LAYLA

Words and Music by
Eric Clapton
and Jim Gordon

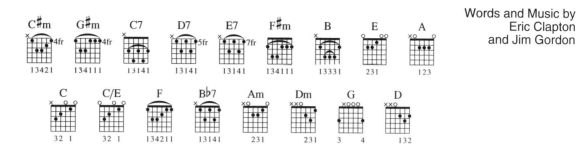
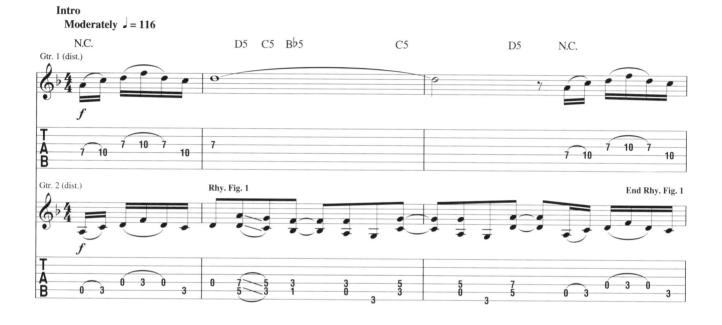
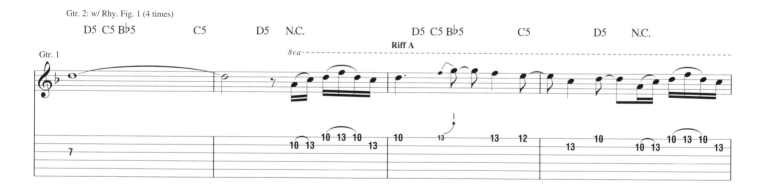
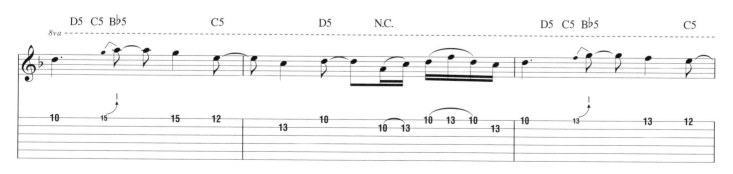

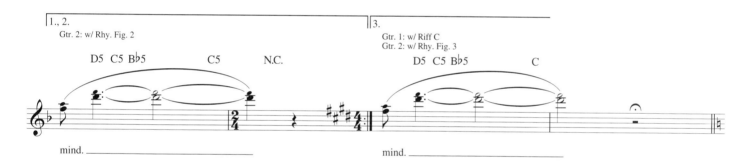
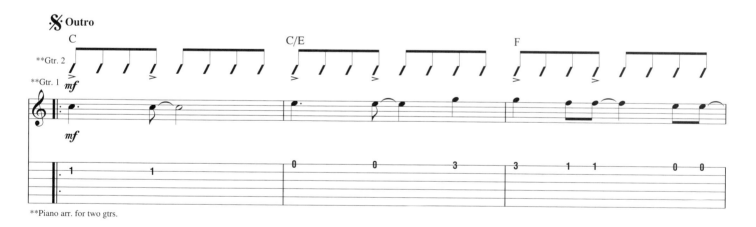
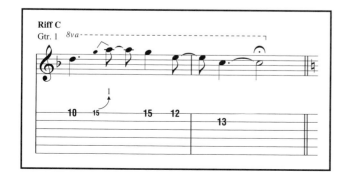

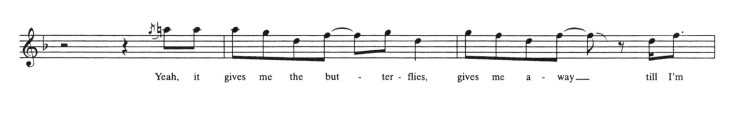

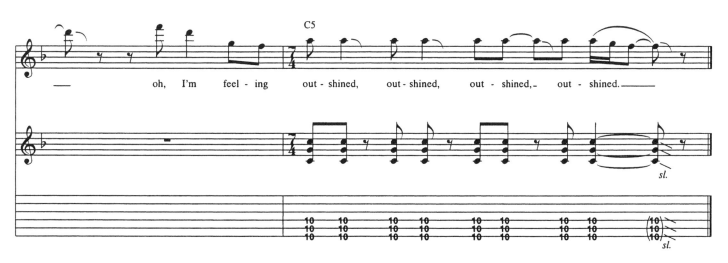
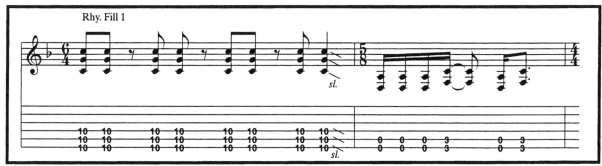

57

PARADISE CITY

Words and Music by
W. Axl Rose, Slash,
Izzy Stradlin', Duff McKagan
and Steven Adler

Additional Lyrics

2. Ragz to richez, or so they say.
   Ya gotta keep pushin' for the fortune and fame.
   It's all a gamble when it's just a game.
   Ya treat it like a capital crime.
   Everybody's doin' their time. *(To Chorus)*

3. Strapped in the chair of the city's gas chamber,
   Why I'm here I can't quite remember.
   The surgeon general says it's hazardous to breathe.
   I'd have another cigarette but I can't see.
   Tell me who ya gonna believe. *(To Chorus)*

4. Captain America's been torn apart.
   Now he's a court jester with a broken heart.
   He said, "Turn me around and take me back to the start."
   I must be losin' my mind. "Are you blind?"
   I've seen it all a million times. *(To Chorus)*

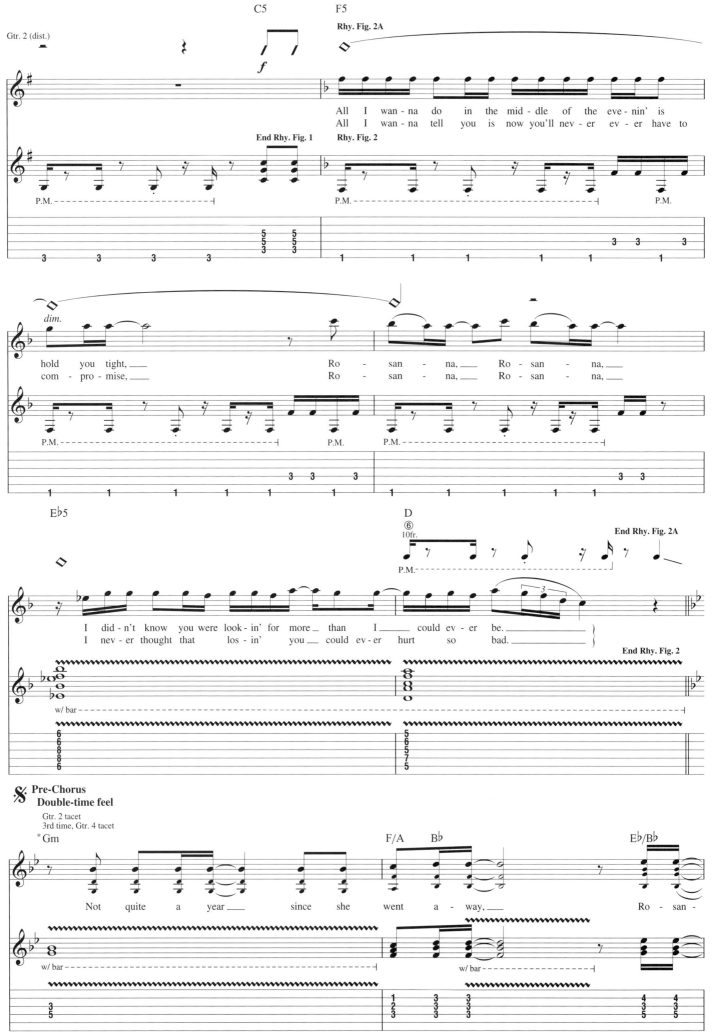

Runnin' With The Devil

Words and Music by
David Lee Roth, Edward Van Halen,
Alex Van Halen and Michael Anthony

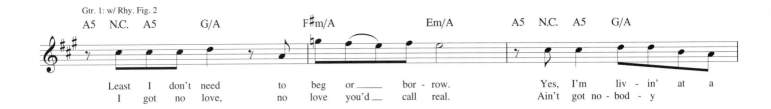

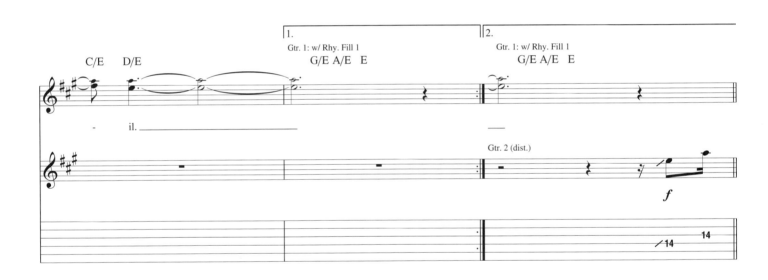
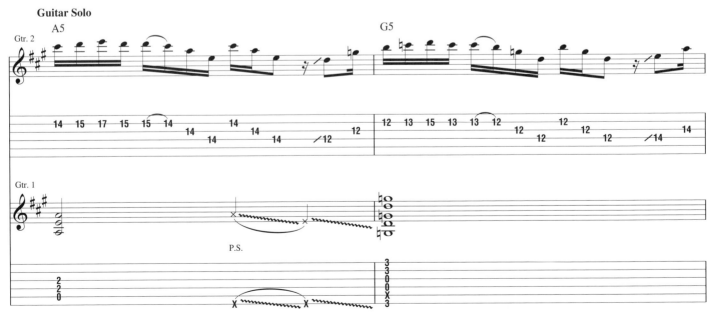

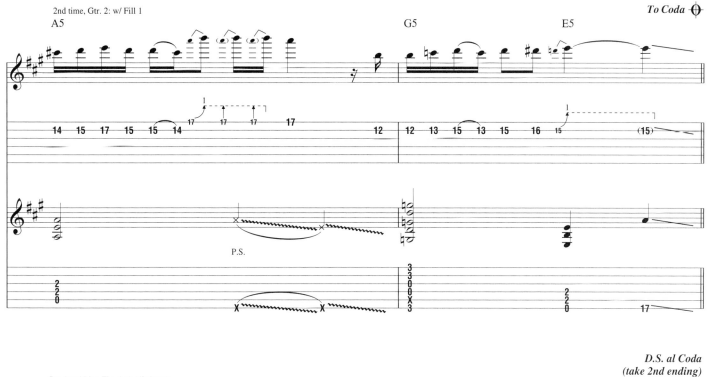

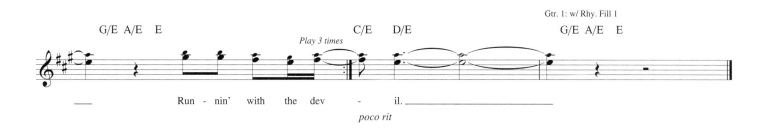

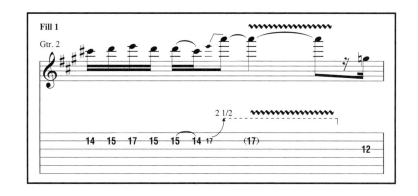

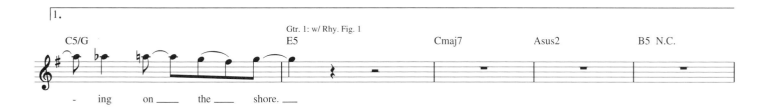
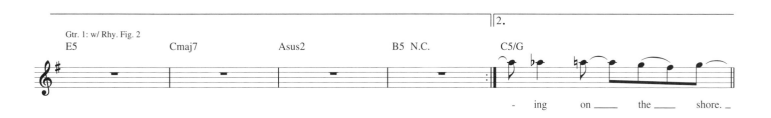

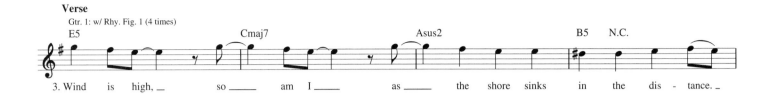
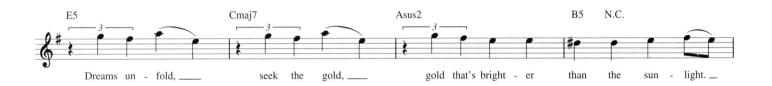
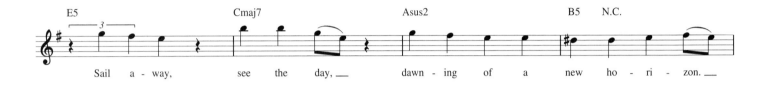
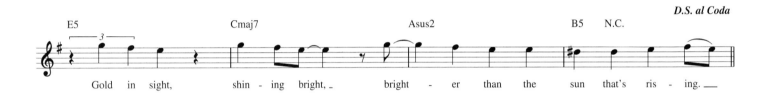
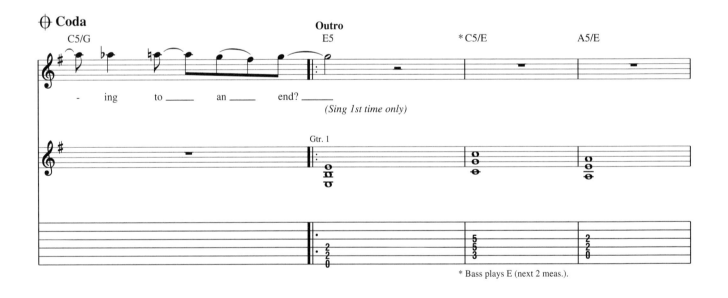
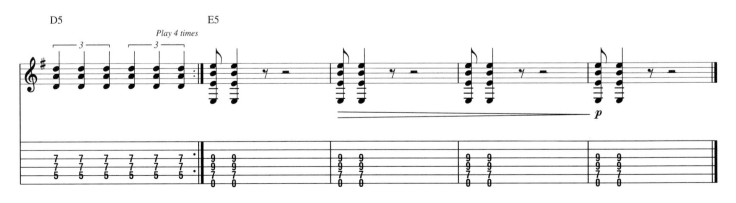

TIGHTROPE

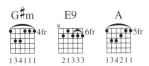

Written by Stevie Ray Vaughan
and Doyle Bramhall

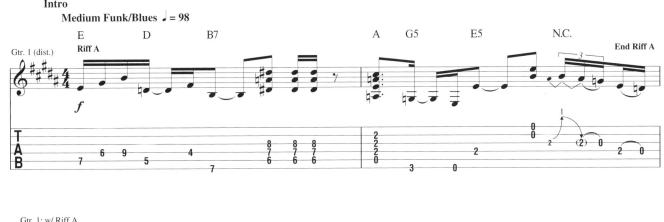

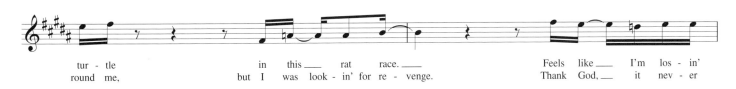

© 1989 RAY VAUGHAN MUSIC (ASCAP), SOBERAY MUSIC (BMI)/Administered by BUG MUSIC and SONGS OF DREAMWORKS (BMI)
Worldwide Rights for SONGS OF DREAMWORKS Administered by CHERRY RIVER MUSIC CO.
All Rights Reserved   Used by Permission

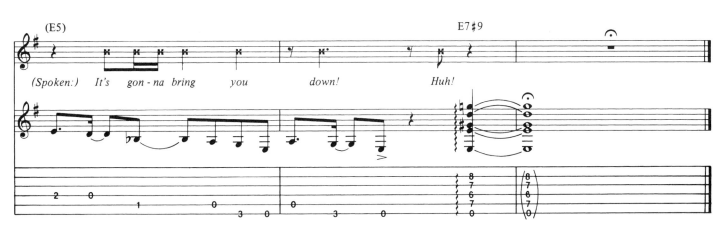

Additional Lyrics

2. Welcome to the jungle, we take it day by day.
   If you want it, you're gonna bleed, but it's the price you pay.
   And you're a very sexy girl who's very hard to please.
   You can taste the bright lights, but you won't get them for free.
   In the jungle. Welcome to the jungle.
   Feel my, my, my, my serpentine.
   I wanna hear you scream!

3. Welcome to the jungle, it gets worse here every day.
   You learn to live like an animal in the jungle where we play.
   If you got a hunger for what you see, you'll take it eventually,
   You can have anything you want, but you better not take it from me.
   In the jungle. Welcome to the jungle.
   Watch it bring you to your sha na na na na na na na na na na na knees, knees.
   I'm gonna watch you bleed! *(To Bridge)*

WALK THIS WAY

Guitar Notation Legend

Guitar Music can be notated three different ways: on a *musical staff*, in *tablature*, and in *rhythm slashes*.

RHYTHM SLASHES are written above the staff. Strum chords in the rhythm indicated. Use the chord diagrams found at the top of the first page of the transcription for the appropriate chord voicings. Round noteheads indicate single notes.

THE MUSICAL STAFF shows pitches and rhythms and is divided by bar lines into measures. Pitches are named after the first seven letters of the alphabet.

TABLATURE graphically represents the guitar fingerboard. Each horizontal line represents a string, and each number represents a fret.

HALF-STEP BEND: Strike the note and bend up 1/2 step.

BEND AND RELEASE: Strike the note and bend up as indicated, then release back to the original note. Only the first note is struck.

HAMMER-ON: Strike the first (lower) note with one finger, then sound the higher note (on the same string) with another finger by fretting it without picking.

TRILL: Very rapidly alternate between the notes indicated by continuously hammering on and pulling off.

PICK SCRAPE: The edge of the pick is rubbed down (or up) the string, producing a scratchy sound.

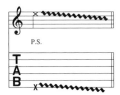

TREMOLO PICKING: The note is picked as rapidly and continuously as possible.

WHOLE-STEP BEND: Strike the note and bend up one step.

PRE-BEND: Bend the note as indicated, then strike it.

PULL-OFF: Place both fingers on the notes to be sounded. Strike the first note and without picking, pull the finger off to sound the second (lower) note.

TAPPING: Hammer ("tap") the fret indicated with the pick-hand index or middle finger and pull off to the note fretted by the fret hand.

MUFFLED STRINGS: A percussive sound is produced by laying the fret hand across the string(s) without depressing, and striking them with the pick hand.

VIBRATO BAR DIVE AND RETURN: The pitch of the note or chord is dropped a specified number of steps (in rhythm) then returned to the original pitch.

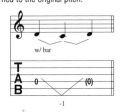

GRACE NOTE BEND: Strike the note and immediately bend up as indicated.

VIBRATO: The string is vibrated by rapidly bending and releasing the note with the fretting hand.

LEGATO SLIDE: Strike the first note and then slide the same fret-hand finger up or down to the second note. The second note is not struck.

NATURAL HARMONIC: Strike the note while the fret-hand lightly touches the string directly over the fret indicated.

PALM MUTING: The note is partially muted by the pick hand lightly touching the string(s) just before the bridge.

VIBRATO BAR SCOOP: Depress the bar just before striking the note, then quickly release the bar.

SLIGHT (MICROTONE) BEND: Strike the note and bend up 1/4 step.

WIDE VIBRATO: The pitch is varied to a greater degree by vibrating with the fretting hand.

SHIFT SLIDE: Same as legato slide, except the second note is struck.

PINCH HARMONIC: The note is fretted normally and a harmonic is produced by adding the edge of the thumb or the tip of the index finger of the pick hand to the normal pick attack.

RAKE: Drag the pick across the strings indicated with a single motion.

VIBRATO BAR DIP: Strike the note and then immediately drop a specified number of steps, then release back to the original pitch.